THE BOOK OF TITLES

MY JOURNEY TO RECOVERY

THE BOOK OF TITLES

MY JOURNEY TO RECOVERY

KEVIN CLARK

Published by Big Shots Publishing
ISBN: 978-1-7330258-3-6

Printed in the United States of America.

DEDICATION

I would like to dedicate this book to all alcoholics and addicts. If you are walking a fine line with nowhere to go, it is not out of reach—God is right there. The more you call him, the more he can hear you.

I love everyone, and I want this book to give at least one person a glimmer of hope.

Never discount the POWER of words

Never underestimate the POWER of God

And always, remember . . .

When you think you have it bad,
someone always has it worse

CONTENTS

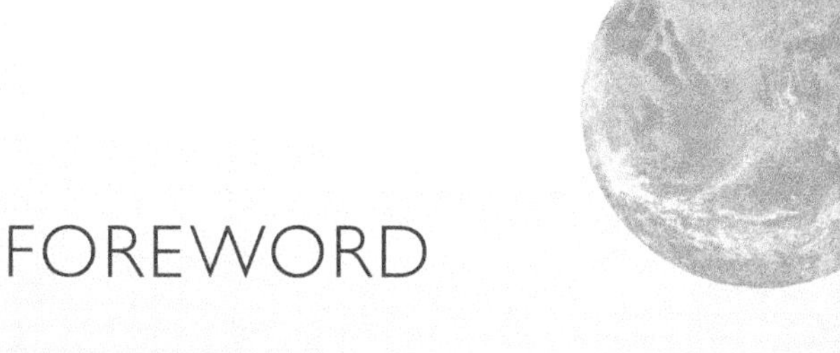

FOREWORD

A MOTHER'S STORY

My son was born October 31, 1979—a Halloween baby. The third of four children—my only son. He was a brown-eyed redhead and a true blessing from heaven. He was an unbelievably good baby—content, seldom cried, and loved being in his car seat. He was my third child in four years, so I kind of needed a break. His car seat fetish, although a bit odd, allowed me the opportunity to take my three children with me whenever I was officiating basketball games to make a little extra money. I am not sure I could get away with these antics today, but it was the 70s, and it seemed to be okay.

We were a career military family. So, we moved every two to three years. This lifestyle is never easy on kids, and it seemed to be extremely stressful for him. It led to a lot of insecurities. For example, when I would be away at night on some type of official function (as an officer's wife), he would call wherever I was three to four times a night to check on when I was coming home. This was before cell phones, so I would always have to tell the host it was probably my son calling. And more often than not, it was. In addition, he constantly chewed holes in the collars of his school shirts. He also had a pretty bad stuttering issue. As his mother, I wish I had been more on top of things then. Maybe I could have calmed some of his fears. I guess I will never really know.

Anyway, by second grade, it was obvious that school was not his thing. In December of that year, his second-grade teacher told me that he could not read. She was so right. At night, we would work so hard, but this reading thing just never really clicked with him. As a teacher, I knew the consequences of being semi-literate, but I guess I figured, if we just kept plowing forward and hoping for the best, it would be alright. After all, he was such a good boy—so kind-hearted, always looking out for the underdog. He would be fine. Besides, I had four children by then, and the daily challenges of being a military-dependent family were at times overwhelming. I was doing the best I could—or so I thought.

By the time my son reached middle school we had moved four times. His dad had done a 13-month unaccompanied tour in Korea, spent most of his so-called time at home being deployed or in the field, and for all practical purposes was an absentee dad. Military life has a way of doing that. My son became increasingly lost and unsure of himself.

In seventh grade, my son became mesmerized with rap music, gangsters, and thugs. He seemed to idolize this way of life and slowly developed an affinity for the excitement and uncertainty of living on the edge. He really wasn't doing anything bad, so I chose to dismiss his attraction to the gangster lifestyle and just chalk it up to adolescence. My oh my, what we tell ourselves in the name of adolescence. Sometimes, I guess, it is just easier for parents to bury their heads in the sand than it is to face the ugly truth. It wouldn't take long for my head to be brutally pried from the sand. My son's lifelong struggle with drugs and alcohol was just on the horizon.

During my son's sophomore year in high school, we moved again. Imagine my shock when one day while I was at my teaching job I got called to the office to take an emergency phone call. It was my 16-year-old son calling me from the Houston, Texas, airport to let me know that he was stuck in the airport with no money. This would have been a concern for any parent. The problem was we lived in Columbus, Ohio, at the time. To this day, I am not really sure how he even got to the Houston airport. I should have realized then that he really had no fears when it came to living on the edge. But, again, I chose the head-in-the-sand approach.

That was a difficult year for him. He didn't fit in with the somewhat cliquish kids in Columbus, Ohio, and school progressively got harder and harder. This was the first time we had not lived on a military installation. The other kids were not like him; they couldn't relate, and he was alone. He cut school almost every day, and if he wasn't sitting alone behind the Meijer getting high, he was riding around in stolen cars with his new-found friends. He ultimately dropped out of high school before his junior year.

By age 20, he was a father and seemed to be turning his life around. He got his GED and decided to join the Army. Unfortunately, that didn't last long because by age 22 he was discharged from the Army for illegal drug use. He then had two sons and a pretty significant drug problem.

For the next several years, his life was a roller coaster—moving fast with lots of ups and downs. It became increasingly harder and harder for him to keep a job. He not only used drugs but also was selling them. His marriage failed, his time with his kids became more strained, and his run-ins with the law became more frequent.

Without really any warning, we (my son and I) found ourselves living the life of not only drug addicts, but of a drug maker and drug dealer. I say we because, during those years, I (the head-in-the-sand lady) became the consummate enabler. Unintentionally, I fueled his drug addiction. I became complicit in his loneliness and his desperate search for self. What a fool I was.

I cannot possibly tell you of all the times I came to his rescue and all the times I tried to reason with him. In my angst to find what was left of my son, I surrendered all rational thought. His addiction consumed me. For me, these were times of absolute hopelessness and futility. I was borderline insane, yet I always clung to the hope—the dream—that my prodigal son would find his way home. He needed something to light his way. Then, one day, he began to talk about his "book of titles."

He said, "Mom, I have been writing down titles for years now. And I think I can make a book out of them."

I was puzzled to say the least, but I asked, "Titles of what?"

He just said, "Titles. I have hundreds of them. I write them all the time."

I wasn't sure if this was the drugs talking or him, but I went along with the idea. By this time, his life had spiraled completely out of control. Sometimes I wouldn't hear from him for weeks or months. I never knew where he was living or if he was even alive. And then, every so often, I would get a call telling me he had to move. He would always ask me to go get his stuff (whatever remained of his possessions). But more importantly, he would tell me to make sure that I got the copies of his titles. I did, and I kept them stored away in a safe place.

Every so often for the next year and half, when he bounced in and out of jail, I would receive an envelope in the mail full of titles. The list grew. Sometimes, late at night when I was wondering where he was, praying that he wasn't dead, I would read them. I laughed. I cried. But always, I prayed for my prodigal son to return.

Then the miracle happened.

In March of 2016, my son's time on the streets finally ran out. He was arrested and sent to jail, and he faced a long list of felony charges. For the next year and a half, I visited him every weekend. Some visits were cordial, and some were downright hostile, but he would always tell me that he had written more titles. He said that he even began to share them with his fellow inmates. "They liked them," he said. "And you know, inmates are a pretty tough bunch to impress." Either way, envelopes filled with titles kept coming from the county jail, and his list continued to grow.

Then, in October of 2017, my son's life of wandering came to an end. He was court-mandated to enroll in a drug-rehabilitation program or face 10 years in prison. He chose rehab. During his road to recovery, he continued to write titles, and he continued to send them to me. The list of titles had taken on a life of its own. It became *The Book of Titles.*

In September 2020, my son will celebrate three years of sobriety.

I know that it is God's grace that saved my son. I know that it is God's grace that saved me. But during those dark, desperate, lonely days when it seemed that I had lost my son forever, I know it was the titles that gave me hope. It was the titles that made me laugh and cry. It was the titles that helped me believe that someday my son would be whole again. For me, this book is not just a book of titles. It is a book of hope—a book of recovery—but most of all, this book is a miracle.

So, please enjoy the titles. Maybe you can find your own miracle in one of them.

PREFACE

BOOK OF TITLES

I am a Halloween baby, born October 31, 1979, in Louisville, Kentucky—a redhead, born with an attitude, if there is such a thing. I have three sisters, a mom, and a dad. My dad was a military man. So, you know what that means—we moved all the time. Mom was a schoolteacher. Sounds like a pretty darn solid life, don't you think? Guess you never know what twists and turns life has in store for you.

Ever since I can remember, I was highly competitive, yet I was always fighting for the underdog. As I look back on it now, I think it was because I *was* one of the underdogs; I just didn't want to admit it. But more importantly, I always dreamed of being successful. Don't we all? I wanted to be the next Michael Jordan or, in my case, the next Tupac Shakur.

Unfortunately, you wouldn't have thought being successful was on my mind given my grades in school. School was hard, really hard, and I was just not willing to put in the work. I became a class clown and even a bully at times. I needed some way to prove myself, and it was obvious it was not going to be in the classroom. I searched for a place where I belonged. It didn't take me long to find it.

By the time I was 15, I had developed a pretty significant weed habit. During my sophomore year in high school we moved again, this time to Columbus, Ohio. Columbus was a tough place. I found it harder and harder to fit in, so weed became my best friend. Instead of going to school, I spent my days sitting alone behind the local Meijer getting high. I dropped out of high school and started running with a really rough crowd. My hopes and dreams of being successful were being hijacked by my illegal drug use. The problem was I just didn't know it, nor did I care. I was on the pathway to something *big*—I could feel it. Funny how we are so easily deceived when we are young.

Living the street life —the glamour, the hip-hop music, the souped-up cars, the rush of living on the edge—that was cool, and that was what I wanted. So, I ventured into the streets. It wasn't long before my weed habit turned to coke. Drugs clutched a hold on my life like a pair of vise grips. I was a pseudo-gangster, pretending I had it all when I really had nothing.

The funny thing was, all the while I was out there, I had this underlying spiritual presence that kept tugging at me, calling me back. Back to where, I didn't know. By this time, I was scared to be me. To be honest, I was not even sure I knew who "me" was anymore. I found myself trying to be someone I wasn't. People-pleasing became a big thing to me. Everybody loved me, or at least that is what I thought. Not too long after my descent into coke, I kind of wised up and realized that this lifestyle was a dead-end street. At this point, I knew I needed a change.

So, I got my GED and then took off for Louisville, Kentucky. I needed a change of scenery. I was only 17 at the time. Louisville was home to me, but with no place really to stay, I slept in my car behind my grandma's house. She would let me use her bathroom and feed me every now and then. Every day she would ask, "Kevin, what are you doing?" And, every day I would tell her, "Don't worry Grandma, I got this." Her response would then be, "Well, I will pray for you." I don't think I did a very good job of convincing her. I'm not really sure I did a very good job of convincing myself either. But I was 17, on my own, and invincible. Eventually, I got a job at a pager and cell phone store. It wasn't very glamorous, but at least I had some money and could stop mooching off of my grandma.

What a life-changer this job turned out to be. That is where *it* happened. I met the love of my life. She was young, beautiful, funny, and living on her own just like me. We were a match made in heaven. We were living for the moment with no real cares in the world, and then things changed. She got pregnant and we had to move back to Columbus, Ohio, to stay with my parents until the baby was born. There I was, 19 years old, still smoking weed, and about to be a father. It was time for another change of course. I joined the Army.

Surprisingly, initially I was a really good soldier. It was hard, but I excelled. I made friends easily. My drill sergeants even liked me—if there is such a thing. Then, without warning, about a year and a half into my enlistment, this gnawing insecurity crept back into my life. I began questioning "me" again. Basic training had taught me that good soldiers know how to assess the enemy and attack. So, I went on the offensive. My weapon of choice was weed. Weed returned with a vengeance, and I didn't care. After all, it was just weed, I told myself. Unfortunately, the Army didn't see it that way.

One day while I was on extra duty awaiting my discharge, the command sergeant major gave me a coin. He said he had never done anything like that before, but he felt he had to because I was always smiling and looking out for my fellow soldiers. He told me I was not only a "good soldier," but more importantly I was a "good person." He said I had a way of bringing light into the darkness. He didn't have to do that. At that moment, I felt that underlying spiritual presence tugging at me again. Too cocky and proud, I ignored the feeling. As I look back on it now, I think God was trying to help me find "me." I just wasn't ready to respond.

I was discharged from the Army, and by this time I was married with two young sons. I moved to Florida and started doing concrete work. That is where I met this Mexican guy. He was like one of the cool gangster guys from the movies. He had a ton of money and plenty of coke to sell. This was the big chance I had been waiting for, I thought. I have to admit I was a bit torn. The insecure, lost "me" was all in, but the married father of two had doubts. I tried to fight the urge, so I continued my concrete work for a short while. Ultimately, the temptation of the street life was just too much. I ended up dealing and using coke again. In no time at all, I had made a lot of money. So eventually, with a car full of coke and money, I moved my family back to Louisville.

When I got to Louisville, I went to my buddy and showed him my pocket full of money and my stash of coke. He laughed and said, "You got the coke, but I have the meth." I asked, "What is that?" He said not to worry and helped me move what I had. He then asked if I wanted to be a part of the action. All I had to do was buy some pseudoephedrine and I would make a ton of money. This time I was all in. He didn't have to ask me twice. This was going to be too easy. And he wasn't wrong—I made great money, or at least that is what I thought. I was living the fast street life and loving it. Maybe I had finally found the "me" I had been looking for.

I guess I kind of knew that this lifestyle wasn't the most reliable for raising a family, so, while being a middleman for meth production, I managed to acquire a job as a plumber's helper. I eventually became a certified plumber. I quickly realized that I loved plumbing almost as much as I loved the thrill of the street life. Foolishly, I thought that I could do both.

But one day I made a life-altering decision. I tried the meth. The sensation was unbelievable. It took away all those old, bad feelings that I had had all my life. I no longer felt like I was not good enough; I wasn't afraid anymore. I finally found "me." This was the "me" I had always been searching for. Life was great, or so I thought.

Shortly after this fatal decision to use meth, I became a father for a third time—to a daughter. At 24 years old, I was a husband, a father of three, a plumber, and a meth addict. Tragically for me, my wife was not willing to live with my addiction, and we split up. I ran wild for about a year.

But much like before, there was this voice calling me back. I realized that I loved my family too much to continue down this destructive path, so I went back to my wife and started plumbing again. I stopped using the meth, but I continued with the weed. Selling weed kept me close to the streets. Every day, the urge for meth viciously haunted my mind. I was able to steer clear of it for several years. I thought I was in control. Hah! What a joke. There is no control when your life is hopelessly and unabashedly tied to drugs.

Life began spiraling downward. My wife and I were just not working out. So, she left, and she took the kids. I was devastated. There I was—alone. I didn't feel sure about myself, and I had that scared feeling again. Desperate for an answer, I turned to meth.

I fell for about five years. Food and money were hard to come by, so I stole from everybody I knew. I was in and out of jail on all kinds of charges—DUI, driving on a suspended license, shoplifting, using, dealing, trafficking, stealing cars. You name it, I did it. I burned every bridge I had. Eventually, I ended up homeless and in all kinds of trouble.

Which brings me to the reason for this book. All the while I was out there, I had this vision of a book of titles. Sometimes, it was the only thing that made sense to me. To be honest, the titles may have been the only thing that kept me alive at times. I began writing titles down on anything I could find and would give them to my mom whenever I could. High and alone in a hotel room, I would write them on hotel stationary. Hungry and cold, living in a car, I would write them on napkins. When I was locked up, I would write them on legal pads and send them to my mom. Sometimes, I even told my cellmates what I was doing. Some of them said I was crazy. But others would say that the idea was pretty awesome. I needed something to believe in.

The last time I got locked up, I spent 18 months in the county jail awaiting my trial date. I was defiant as ever. I fumed as I knew I was being screwed by the legal system. I couldn't wait to get out and return to the drugs. Eighteen months is a long time. So, either out of desperation or boredom, or just acting a fool, or unknowingly investing in a yet-to-be seen miracle, I continued to write my titles. My mother visited every weekend. We would occasionally talk about the titles, and I would tell her of my dream to make a book of titles. Every so often, I mailed her an envelope postmarked from the county jail containing my handwritten titles. She meticulously safeguarded my titles as if they were sacred property. *The Book of Titles* was my dream, but I know now it was her hope.

Finally, about a month before my sentencing date, I knew I was done. I cried to my father, God, to please save me, to help me. I wanted out. And you know what? God answered my prayers. At my sentencing hearing, the judge gave me an option of a court-mandated rehab program or ten years in a prison. I went to rehab on October 18, 2017, straight from jail.

During my time in recovery, I continued to write my titles. The more sober I became, the more my vision of sharing my titles began to feel like a reality. I have been clean and sober for almost three years now. These days I dedicate myself to God to living how the program taught me to live.

I waited a long time to be the person I am today. I waited a long time to be the "me" I was meant to be. God is real and forgiving. He is my life today. These days I work hard plumbing, spending time with my family and living a life free of drugs one day at a time. I am so grateful to be alive. I am so grateful for the gift of the titles.

Just as I think the titles were God's gift to me, I would like to share this gift with you. They may not help to free you from addiction, but I truly hope my titles help calm you when you need to relax. I hope they inspire you when you need to imagine. I hope they reassure you when you need to persevere. I hope they bring a chuckle to your soul when you need to laugh. But most of all, I hope they give you faith when you need to believe.

My name is Kevin Clark, and this is my *Book of Titles*.

CHAPTER 1

LIVING THE FAST LIFE

My Buddy the Whale

I Kidnapped a Whale

The Cat That Poured Concrete

Translucent Pig

Karma Quilt

Larry the Giraffe

The Stone Cat

The House of Bones

Stuck in a Bubble

Night of the Campfire

Nightmare Fishing Trip

Ride the River

The Dam of Survival

Chat in a Box

The Rich Homeless Man

The Last Time

Live to Die

The Sheep with Fangs

Pedro the Billy Goat

The Glass Future

Crying Leaves

Cut by the Grass

Long Lonely Nights

Drowned by Your Presence

Talking Hamster

Too Much Time

Story Watch

Looking Towards the Sky

I Wish I Were an Ant

I Want to Be a Bird

Crooked Power

The Boy Who Always Lost

New Boot, Eric

Captain Chapter

Moving Again

Keeping Results Clean

Moving with Music

Mud in My Cup

Eyeballs on the Stop Sign

The Groundhog Band

Fell into Her Eyes

Jumped Out of the Picture

Dedicated to . . .

Symbols from Pictures

Real Dreams

Seemed So Real

Screaming Chills

My Talking Baseball Bat

Universe Life

Two Cats Collide

The Running Bowling Ball

Star Clouds

Energy Star

Watching You

Ocean Blues

The Crying Ocean

Racing through the Desert

History Time Watch

Fell into the Clock

Walked into the Timing

Eyes through the Window

Gold Ocean

Pet Marshmallows

Camera by Life

Whispering Grass

Jumped into It

The Talking Gun

Sinkhole Heaven

Invisible Cat

Skydive Journey

Missed My Turn

The Worst Laugh

Hypnotizing Laugh

Walking Time

Desert Battle

The Day is Over

Listen in Silence

The Chicken That Laid Golden Eggs

Titles Falling from the Tree

CHASING DRUGS LIKE A DREAM

The Singing Trees

Diving through Life

The Singing Hamster

My Turtle Wears Sunglasses

Hearing Old Voices

Turtle Eyes

Caught in an Avalanche

Scratches on the Wall

Scribbled a Picture

Star Hopping

Mockingbirds Talk

Life as a Shadow

Songs of Choice

The Calm Winds

My Talking Flower

Nighttime Stuck

The Screaming Apple

Legend of a Cowboy

Clock Hand Wisdom

Golden Apartment

Candle Dreams

Light up the Sky

Working Candles

Blank Walk

Screaming Peace

Walking since the 80s

Power by Water

Baby Olympics

Baby Scuba Diver

Brand New Window

The Diary Telephone

The Lay Down

Watching the Rain

Special Times

Ant Prom

Stuck in Me

Scuba Diving with Ants

Mind of Gold

Pizza Delivery Murder

Silent Voices

Border Escape

Flew Off

Memory of Before

Secret Knife

Moved by the Storm

Whispering Butterflies

Struck by Feelings

Deep Walk

The Man Outside

Top Survivors

Grandfather Ant

Run Away Escape

Train Tracks

Path to . . .

Invisible I Am

Movie Life

Lightning Strike

Talking Money

Here We Go

Lost in the Desert

CHAPTER 3

HIGH-SPEED PURSUIT

Lost in the Woods

The Talking Alligator

My Best Friend the Ant

Fast Life

Blink of the Tie

Music Man

Adopted by Drugs

Pain That Filled

Snow Leaves

The Cell Phone

Roller Coaster

Life as an Ant

Dream Chimes

Life as a Chess Piece

Silent Whispers

Tickle the Water

Fish Bag

Why First

Two Feathers

Please the Crowd

Turn Yourself Around

Blemishing Roots

Deep Sea Wonders

Back from the Life

Living Motions

Bless the Alphabet

Secretive Scoring

Diving Board Wisdom

Life Blindfolded

Miniature Octopus

Ever Fought an Octopus

Blood Line

Measure It

Money Can't Buy Freedom

Image of a Lawyer

Hotel Cost

Dinosaur Path

Running Up

Money Time

Stop Watch

Night Calls

Lights at Night

Love You Triangle

Kill Sleep

Simmering Money

Sinkholes

Lightning from Me

Keep Me

The Kitchen

The Milkman

Lightning Shock

Tornado Thoughts

Ice Fishing Journey

Igloo Mountains

Master Time

Ask, You Might Receive

My Biggest Fan the Ant

The Blind Witness

The First Day

Miniature People

Voices in the Air

Submarine Mission

Batter Number Four

Final Seconds

The Talking Bowling Ball

The Sit Down

Talking Raindrops

Grandfather Clock Memories

Lost in the Camera

Talking Shoes

My Pet Giraffe

Born in the Ocean

The Man with No Name

Hearing the Whispers

Test Button

Marshmallow Sea

The Happy Captain

Life Under Water

Super Outfit

Rainy Forest

True Blessings Come

Love Everything

CHAPTER 4

STUCK ONCE AGAIN

Never Showed Up

Mini Hamster

Memory Machine

I Can Move Time

Born into Quicksand

Sinking Ship

The Haunted Bus

The Ghost Storm

Glowing Tree

Mr. Cam, May I?

Life in Black and White

The Blind Wizard

Treasure Hunt

Time Me

The Gift of Danger

The Explosions

Mountain Walk

Poisonous Kool-Aid

Hawk Life

Lost in the Crowd

Memory Loss

No More

It's Time

I'll Time You

Here We Come

Invisible Stage

Life as a Shoe

Life as a Shovel

Tied Up

Broke the Earth

Keep Spinning

Universe Mountains

Drowned in Snow

Mountain Slide

Under Current

The Talking Infinite

The Morning

My Pet Lightning Bug

Drinking Underwater

Manic Hat

I Have Seen You Before

The Meltdown

Skyscraper Heaven

Butterfly Season

My Sister

My Pet Butterfly

Hearing Whispers

The Talking Balloon

The Balloon Ride

Cowboy Ranch

Stuck in the Desert

The Knife Man

Lotto Run

Memories as a Cat

My Talking Cat

Spiders Are Moving

Colors Are Memories

The Known Secret

The of Nothing

Life as a Board Game

CHAPTER 5

THANK GOD FOR PAPER AND PEN

Super Kid

Super Mini Kitten

Captain Lewis

Starving for Fun

Screaming Winds

Marshmallow Palace

Three Too Many

Danger's Peace

Untamable

Screaming Out

The Talking Christmas Tree

Died Happy

Witness to a Miracle

Ice Skating on the Ocean

Trail to Happiness

Talking in Different Tones

Message from the Sky

Blinded in a Crash

Woke up Blind

The Happiest Paralyzed Man

Hollow Bullets

Swords against Guns

Dogs versus Cats

Day of Survival

Never Doubt It

Looking Through You

The Talking Apples

Under Me Is?

Lightning Cries

Midnight Dreams

Answer to It All

Just Using It Don't Cost Nothing

Ghost Forest

Invisible Horses

Baseball Dream Glove

Baseball Bingo Games

Frost on My Windshield

Tall Women

Dancing Horses

Life as a Movie

Penalty of Driving

Ran into My Twin

Angels Next to You and Me

Deaf by Thunder

The Earthquake

Enhanced Milkshake

Looking Down From

The Tip Toes

Drowned in Oil

Mixed Up

Class Clown

Electric Man

Born in the Sky

Odd Ball

Haven't Seen You since Last Time

Last Choice

This Time Around

Healthy Numbers

Great Odds

Chance Taker

Fall before the Rise

Dark Highway

CHAPTER 6

MOVING AGAIN

Broke Down on the Highway

Blind Hitchhiker

Memories of My Present Life

My Pet Dinosaur

Sleigh Ride

Wrapped Up

Personality Hat

Drowned in the Ocean

In Love with a Mermaid

Windmill City

Living through Music

Windmill Time Machine

Thoughts from the Lightning

Gotta Start Somewhere

Dream Titles

Skateboard Heaven

The Bomb Threat

Looking Forward

Stuck in the Circle

Master Strategy

Campfire

Mr. Pleasure

Laser Eyesight

Star Race

Turtle Sports

The Dog Race

Amazing Life

Zoo Break

Captain Horseman

Ocean Travel

Running Still

Mystery Curtains

Lifelong Ride

Reading Between the Lines

Shark Fishing Adventure

Riding Ants

Waterfall Man

Ocean Travel

Mystery Curtains

Lifelong Ride

Walk off a Cliff

Inside the Bomb

The Clapping Ants

Similar to Me

Purple Waters

Laughing Ants

Crushed by the Thunder

Taught by the Birds

Flocking Family

High Power Living

Moved into the Wild

Now or Never

Sinking in the Concrete

High Power Living

Adventure Cravings

Ringing Bells

Joy Brings Me

Cornfield Blessings

One More Move

Seems Simple

Raining Gold

Finishing Titles

Stories from the Titles

Publishers Dream

Big Finish

Talking Pictures

Emotions of Pictures

Ice Skater

Snow Border

Skateboarder Olympics

Skater's Nightmare

Skating Ring Murder

Missing in Action

Everyone Loves Me

CHAPTER 7

TRAVELING LIKE THE WEATHER

I Love to Love

Running on Fumes

Pinocchio's Parents

Mountain Climbing

Path to Danger

Death Anniversary

Owls Follow Me

Bluegrass Mountaintops

Making Bond

Dream Programmer

The Curing Raindrops

Trampoline of Clouds

Star #64995

Study Eviction

Bound by Water

Disc Mystery

Avalanche Challenge

Melting Mountains

Running from Yourself

My Shadow and Me

The Sunniest Night

Falling into It

The Puzzle Follows Me

Screaming Silent

Animal Man

Slow Tide

Generally Gross

Applauding Clouds

Winning Is Losing

Losing Is Winning

Jumping from Cloud to Cloud

My Eyes Are in the Future

Night Vision Eyesight

Wisdom from the Clouds

Fire at the Bottom of the Ocean

Talking Fish

Wisdom from the Sky

My Best Friend is a Goldfish

The Singing Catfish

The Yelling Bluegill

Wondering Why

The Invisible Outfit

Pleasured Clothes

Wow, It's Mine

My Car is Moody

Riding Clouds

Roller Coaster from Heaven

Run with the Angels

Hop in the Car, Man

If You Want to Get Bigger

The Candy Store

The Halloween Baby—Me

Should I Be Bigger

Rainstorms Under Water

Life in the Fast Lane

Evil Sunglasses

The Dissing Hole

Sinkhole in the Basement

Lost in the Sauce

Miracle Day

Long Days

Empty Moments

Music Box

Music Miracle

Positive Talk

Lose Your Way

Lost Look

Crazed Bus Driver

Haunted Bus

Stuck in the Middle

Turning Back

Keep It Spinning

Memories of the Past

P. D. Saved Me

Seconds Away

The Schoolteacher

Ghost High School

Walking Home

Add Me In

Secret Story

Trampoline to the Top

Lemonade Stand

CHAPTER 8

I DON'T NEED HELP

Hidden Message

Talking Shoes

Stopwatch

Swimming with the Sharks

Born Rich

The Red House

The Chosen

He Is Special

Time Catcher

Slow Music

The Haunted Dance

The Haunted Kool-Aid Stand

The Book Titles

Struck by God

Shockwave Heaven

The Day of the Earthquake

Church Hill Downs

Lost in the Woods

Looking for Love

Double Team

Sound Waves from Space

Space Below

Home Run Derby

Special Teams

Angel Within

The Redhead

My Puddle Is Drying Up

Happy Tears

Rhythm Naturally

Sleepwalking

Night Life

My Talking Night Light

The Creepiest Move Ever

The Dancing Salt and Pepper Shakers

Lightning Bug Heaven

Running From . . .

Lightning Bug Family

The Super Trampoline

Swallowed by Pain

My Own Time

Keep It If You Can

Good Sense of Time

Eyeballs Watching Me

Exercise Kings

The Realist Dream

The King's Palace

Believe It Can Happen

Best Family

Golden Path

Messenger through the Radio

Fast Ball

The Winning Shot

Robbery Heaven

Bike Race

Classic Cars

The Mystery Letter

The Machine Tent

Shoe Seller

Come IOU

Day of Release

Walking Scared

Roller Coaster Nightmare

CHAPTER 9

I CAN SEE THE SUN COMING OVER THE MOUNTAINTOPS

The Hot Air Balloon Trip

Being Watched

Winners' Circle

One Day

Woke up Somewhere Else

The Basement of the Basement

Scattered Rainstorms

New Start

The Fill-Up

Small Clouds

Life as a Tree

The Pedaling Bike

Rojo—Español

The Growing Stuffed Animal

I'm Ready—Are You?

Life Underwater

My Best Friend Can Swim in a Fish Tank

The Talking Silverware

The Fastest Growing Grace Ever

The Door to the Other Side

Sinking Puddle of Water

Bumblebee All-Star Game

The Day I Saw a Man Air-Assaulting from a Bumblebee

The Creepiest Stairs Ever

My Favorite Star

The Talking Night

Creepy Windstorm

My Best Friend, the Tornado

The Money Cloud

One Day Highways Went on Strike

The Swinging Bat

The Baseball That Won the Game

The Loudest, Deadest Crowd Ever

The Foggy Basement

Lego City

The Ringing Telephone

Hallway to Success

Walking Dreamer

Cloudy City

Never-Ending Night

Chasing My Shadow

My Best Friend, the Shadow

Ant City

Magical Snow

Dry Rain

The Helicopter with Its Own Mind

Swamp Life

My Pet Crocodile

Talking Zoo

Following Clouds

Trust in Life

Far Away

Come See My Car

Dark Night

Sunny Night

Shining Star

Talking Walls

The Talking Bathroom

Romantic Park

Coldest Summer Ever

Muscle Cars on the Go

Cars with Feelings

CHAPTER 10

STARS DO TALK

Help is on the Way

No Speed Limit

Secret Stories

Talkative Birds

My Pet is Crazy

Best Days of My Life

Thank You for This Day

Funny People

Born Tiny

The Talking Infant

My Angel is Close

Roads Out of My Doors

I Cry Diamonds

Talking Farm

Storm Chaser

Living Dreams

Every Thought Became Reality

Sword Fighters

Wildfire Fighters

Life as an Eagle

High-Speed Chase

Recovery Act

The Hundred Hallways

The Haunted School

Singing Goldfish

Rough Tides

Stuck in a Hurricane

Walk to Home

No Rules

Scoring Point

Life as a Lifeguard

Life as a Beach Guard

Love for Stray Animals

My Talking Chicken

My Talking Cow

My Talking Farm

After Dad Died I Understood

After Grandpa Died I Could Hear Animals

The Merry-Go-Round

The Spinning Merry-Go-Round

My Talking Farm

Path to the Trail

Lost on a Camping Trip

Lost in the Talking Forest

The Sinkhole

Fire Ant Army

Life as an Insect During Fire

Fire Wild

Wild Fire

The Boss of Fire

Hellfire

Fire Underneath

Stretching Clouds

Fire Rain

The Pet Groomer

The Floating Umbrella

Talking Waves

Talking Beach

My Sandcastle Became Real

Glowing Water

Flying Cars

The Pet Groomer

The Shoes That Walk on Water

Reach Out

Falling from Space

Earthquake Century

Hottest Days

Clock Time

Small Chance

Fall Back

Straight Line I'm On

Walk Don't Run

Drowning Swimming Pool

Creepy Water

Poison in the Water

My Pet Shark

My Pet Elephant

My Pet Crocodile

My Pet Owl

My Pet Owl Stutters

My Pet Alligator Is So Smart

Shaking Hands

CHAPTER 11

IT'S TIME TO LEARN Y'ALL

Life Under Crumbs

History Alive

The Perfect Plan

Mechanic Angels

Talking Under Water

Cool Breeze in the Summer

Watch the Broom

Witch's House

Running with the Witches

I Miss Me

The Complimentary Mirror

Concrete Shoes

Moving Every Other Year

Life as an Army Brat

When I Got Back

Born Blind

Born Deaf

Born Dead

Zombie World on Mars

Mr. Stretch

Platinum Dreams

Skyscraper Heavens

On Top of Chicago

Winds from the Ocean

Summer Camp

Winter Camp

Dance with Me

Unfrozen Background

Life as a Flower

Wind through Your Heart

Pain Driver

Motivation by God

Benjamin Moves

The Lonely Park

Can I Come Back?

I Did It

Look at Me Now

Space Active

Animal Intuition

Experienced

Doing Right Is Better

Never Say Never

You Can Do It

Parachute Didn't Open

Life Is Free

Follow Me

Sled Wednesday

Skiing on a Haunted Mountain

Midnight Skiing

I Love My Nephew

Kids Are Light

Nature Man

Superpowers

Born in an Accident

Morning Fog

When It Rained for a Year

The Insects All-Star Game

Day Shift

The Creepiest Stairs Ever

The Talking Basement

The Talking Night

The Longest Day

I Was So Small I Could Fly on a Bumblebee

THANK YOU FOR TIME STUCK

The Kool-Aid Volcano

The Kool-Aid Sea

Running Money

The Screaming Wind

The Talking Thunderstorm

My Best Friend is Mother Nature

Quicksand Beach

Sinking Mountain

Rising Sea

My Car That Drove Itself

The Emotional Car

I Woke up Speaking Spanish

The Ant Army

The Chasing Water

Catch Me If You Can

Is It Ever Going to Stop Raining?

The Yelling Woods

The Day Tanks Took Over

United We Came

Fell, but Got Up

Try and Stop Me

Creepiest Stairs

The Ant Government

Owl Family

Watch Out I Am in Motion

Black or White

The Jumping Rope

Diamond Beach

Smiles That Lead to Dreams

Overcast Days

What, Where, Why, Who

The Whispering Water

Talking Lakes

Fastest Shoes Ever

The Amazing Toothpaste

Starting at the Finish Line

Beginning to End

Imaginary Notebook

The Day Everybody Became Animated

My Space Journey

No Gravity

Living on Stars

Life after Death

Time Dangles

Super Paints

Tornado at the Bottom of the Ocean

Gold Stream

Gold Streaming from the Mountains

The Golden Brain

English Bulldog Family

Spanish Talking Ants

The Pizza Deliverer

I Love My Dad

The Camping Trip

The Night Before

Walking Up

Walking Across the Old Bridge

Separation of Me

My Ghost

The Shaking Bridge

The Whispering City

Nightmares Awake

Lego City Life

Master Man

Magic Sprinkle

Thunderstorm of the Nights

Earthquake That Cried

Foggy Sun

CHAPTER 13

THE POWER OF PRAYER

Sinking Puddle

Sinking Mattress

The Tallest Tree

A Baseball with Its Own Mind

Rebelling Stars

The Deepest Pool

Runaway Escape

The Train Tracks

Path to?

Invisible I Am

Movie Life

Fast-Talking Money

Early-Morning Dew

Here We Go

Fast Life

Blink of an Eye

Adopted by Drugs

Pain That Filled

Snow Leaves

The Cowboy's Pistol

Golden Bullet

The Cadence

My Best Mile

Climb to the Top

The Deepest Sinkhole

Shallow Treasure

Treasure That Washed Ashore

I Hear You

The Dialing Telephone

Trying to Skip Frequency

Thirsty Water

Running Safe

The Shooting Gun

Fire That Got Fueled by Water

Jump Start

Kiss to Heaven

Fire on Top of the Mountain

I Am on Fire

Sounds from the Clouds

Sounds from the Sky

Happy Nights

Kissing Clouds

Screaming Nights

The First Day

Miniature People

Voices in the Air

Submarine Mission

The Final Seconds

The Sit Down

Talking Raindrops

Money Time

The Backwards Stopwatch

Night Calls

Kill Sleep

Screaming Money

Keep Me

CHAPTER 14

I LOVE CLEAR VISION

Tornado Thoughts

The Kitchen

The Milkman

Crying Stars

Ice Fishing Journey

Igloo Mountain

Master Time

Treasure Hunt

The Gift of Danger

The Explosion

Mountain Walk

Magical Kool-Aid

Sleepless Nights

Lost in the Crowd

Memory Loss

No More

I'll Time You

Here We Come

Invisible Stage

Talking Shoes

Life as a Shoe

Tied Up

Broke the Earth

Keep Spinning

Universe Mountains

Mountain Slide

Undercurrent

Measure Me

Crystal Says No

Tug-of-War Battle

Sidewalk to Heaven

The Cliff

Pretty Voices

Tickle Me Water

Bless the Alphabet

Secretive Scoring

Diving Board Wisdom

Life Blindfolded

Miniature Octopus

Ever Fought an Octopus?

Measure It

Score I Won

Traffic Lights On

Money Can't Buy Freedom

Image of a Lawyer

Hotel Cost

Dinosaur Path

Running Up

Lost in the Camera

My Pet Giraffe

Test Button

Marshmallow Sea

The Happy Captain

Life Underwater

Super Outfit

Rainy Forest

True Blessings Come

Love Everything

Lost in Time

Time Scope

Memory Machine

I Can Move Time

Sinking Ship

The Haunted Bus

The Ghost Storm

Glowing Tree

CHAPTER 15

WAKING UP WITH A PURPOSE

The Blind Wizard

Sitting on the Tracks

Invisible Train

The Talking Infinite

The Morning

My Pet Lightning Bug

Magic Hat

The Melt Down

Butterfly Session

The Knife Man

The Blue Book

People Watching

Lotto Run

Memory as a Cat

My Talking Cat

Spiders are Moving

The Diver

Jumped to the Moon

Planet Movement

Toothbrush Moment

Invisible Wall

My Pet Stars

Star Races

He Made Earth

Collapses

The Broken

Memories Have Arrived

Bless Thanksgiving

Crying Leaves

Talking Leaves

Day of Survival

Bird Length

Life Underground

Flying with the Ocean

Flying with the Birds

President Benefits

The Path

Mad Birds

Helicopter Ride

Colors Are My Life

The Known Secret

Super Kid

Super Mini Kitten

The Captain of Miracles

Starving for Sun

Screaming Winds

Marshmallow Palace

One Too Many

Hostile Peace

Untamable Thoughts

Real Match Box

Sorrow Is Here

I'm Owned by Time

No Wishes

Energy from Space

He Knows

I Did It

Mirror Talk

Careless Time

Sandy Days

Computer Person

Midnight Memories

Beautiful Showers

Look of Judgement

Miracle Smile

Blind Killer

Window Vision

Sinking Thoughts

Last Chance

This Time Around

Healthy Numbers

Great Odds

Chance Taker

True Atmosphere

Scheduled Day 088

Fall Before the Rise

Dark Highway

Sadness in the Light

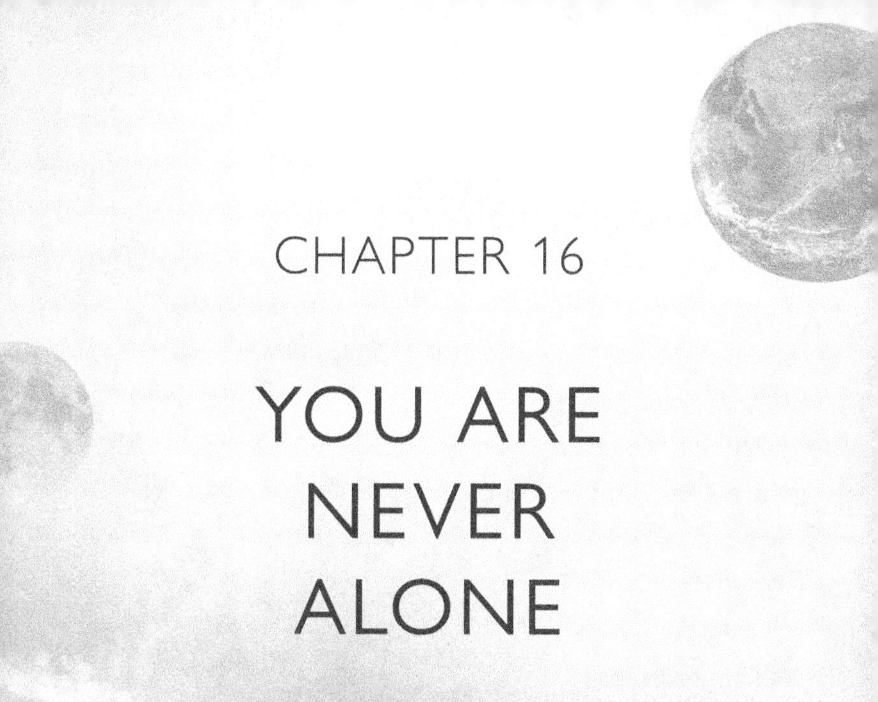

CHAPTER 16

YOU ARE NEVER ALONE

Memories of My Future Life

Anger from the Clouds

Scared to Walk

Baseball Dream Stadium

Baseball Dugout Games

Frost on My Windshield

Tall Women

Dancing Horses

Life as a Mailbox

Penalty of Driving

Ran into My Twin

Angels Next to You

Angels Next to Me

Poison's Breakfast

Too Slow for Lightning

Deaf by Thunder

The Earthquake's Voice

Enhanced Milkshake

Looking Down From

The Tip Toes

Drowned in Oil

Mixed Up

The Class Clown's Book

Electric Man

Born in Heaven

Odd Ball

Haven't Seen You since Last Time

Looking Up

Can't Believe I Found You

Smarty the Ruthless Cat

Witness to a Miracle

Dancing on the Ocean

The Happiest Dead Man

The Ocean Versus the Desert

Homeless for a Moment

CHAPTER 17

MY FATHER'S WORDS, NOT MINE

Smiling Scarecrows

The Night of the Orange

The Talking Apples

Under Me Is?

Lightning Cries

Midnight Dreams

Answer to It All

Just Cuz It Don't Cost Nothing

Finishing Titles

The Titles' Secrets

Writers' Dreams

Impossible Finish

Broken Pictures

The Pictures' Hands

The Blind Artist

Puzzled by Words

Reading Between the Lines

Ice Skater

Snowboarder

Skate Nightmare

Nobody Loves Me

I Love to Laugh

Running on Fumes

Pinocchio's Grandparents

Mountain Climbing

Path to Danger

Choice from Another Mind

Icicle Death

Death Anniversary

Owls Follow Me

Bluegrass Mountain Tops

Making Bond

Shark Fishing Adventure

Riding Ants

The Souls Have Returned

Walk Off a Cliff

Inside the Bomb

The Clapping Ants

The Laughing Ants

Similar to Me

Purple Waters

Crushed by Thunder

Caught with the Birds

Flocking Family

High Power Living

Moved into the Wild

Now or Never

Sinking in the Concrete

Dark Days

Power Said

Adventure Cravings

Ringing Bells

Joy Brings Me

Cornfield Blessing

One More Move

Seems Simple

Raining Gold

Dream Titles

Looking Forward

Stuck in the Circle

Lost on a Road Trip

Having It All

Shock Treatment

Master Strategy

The Noticed

Kidnapped by the Moon

Amazing Life

Ocean Trail

Running Still

Mystery Curtains

Lifelong Ride

My Journey through the Titles

ACKNOWLEDGEMENTS

I would like to thank the following people:

Judge Barry Willett, the judge who mandated me to rehab.
Terry Moody.
The Commitment House.
Dawaun, the voice of God to all us recovering addicts.

And a special thank you to all the following people who never gave up on me:

My mom, who never gave up
on me—ever—no matter what.
My sister, Christine Urbancik, who
always had open arms and true care for me.
Katie Clark and Kelly Clark, my sisters.
My kids, Kevin, Trenton and Taegan.
Rhea Cecil, my partner in life since I recovered.
Bob Scott, the baddest plumber I know.
John Urbancik, a brother from another mother.
Aunt Anne and Uncle Tom, I love you guys.
Uncle Kirk, thank you.
Aunt Amy, you came to my court dates.
Aunt Michael, you are the coolest.
Angie Bowman, I love you.
Trey, Alexis, and Damian Bowman, I love you guys.
In memory of Joe Bowman—I will always miss
and love you. One of my best friends, ever.

www.ingramcontent.com/pod-product-compliance
Lightning Source LLC
LaVergne TN
LVHW051124080426
835510LV00018B/2218

9781733025836